LET AUGMENTED REALITY
CHANGE HOW YOU READ A BOOK

With your smartphone, iPad or tablet you can use the **Neighbur Vue** app to invoke the augmented reality experience to literally read outside the book.

neighbur

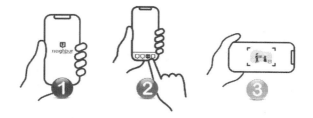

1. Notice the spelling: download the **Neighbur Vue** app from the Apple App Store or Google Play (hint: searching "Vue Neighbur" works well)

2. Open and select the (vue) option

3. Point your lens at the full image with the and enjoy the augmented reality experience.

Go ahead and try it right now with the Hasmark Publishing International logo.

Once the content begins, click the 'UNLOCKED' icon to then lock the content onto your phone.

ENDORSEMENTS

"Nigella Lawson (famous food writer and TV cook), called house-wives swamped with home duties Domestic Goddesses. Now, Pauline Irene Stacey cleverly shows them the way forward. After reading this practical manual, you will ask yourself if house-cleaning will ever become an Olympic sport. *Ready, set, go!* with Pauline."

—David Grodski,
International bestselling author of
The Wisdom of Wellness

"Pauline Irene Stacey delivers a comprehensive, systematic strat-egy to cleaning, guaranteed to give you more time to do what you love while enjoying a clean home. As a mother and wife with a challenging career in healthcare, I am delighted that Pauline has written her practical, time-saving, simple cleaning methodology to share with the world. I have been following her proven system for almost 30 years. Whether you are looking for more time for your family or yourself or to save thousands of dollars on cleaning services, I guarantee her easy-to-follow techniques will give you hours back to your week, and you'll love the look and feel of a professionally cleaned home."

—Jessica Gagnon

"Pauline says that she will rescue you from the drudgery of cleaning. I did not believe in the probability of it ever happening. However, Pauline made it possible through a process of science and psychology. I tried it, and it worked. Her fourth choice together with a positive attitude and energy simplify the task and give you great pride in sharing your acquired knowledge with your friends and family. This book is a must read. We all need an uplifting process for every activity related to the comfort of our lives."

—Muriel Prior,
International bestselling author of
The Best Move of Your Life

"Here's my thing, my rating system is the 4 E's: entertaining, empathetic, engaging, and educational. I am all about cleaning, and Pauline Irene Stacey has written a great book on taking the stress out of cleaning. It is engaging and educational. It will enlighten and entertain you. It gets the four Es."

—Brian Sebastian,
Host of *Movie Reviews & More*

"If you think you have no time to clean, Pauline Irene Stacey will ensure that you reclaim your lost hours of the day with her expert cleaning advice. *No Time to Clean? Listen to Pauline!* puts power back into the hands of her reader by encouraging a shift in mindset and the use of simple but effective cleaning tips and tricks."

—Peggy McColl,
New York Times bestselling author

NO TIME TO
Clean?
LISTEN TO
Pauline!

A manual-style handbook in an easy-to-read format with step-by-step basic instructions and hacks to perform weekly cleaning chores in three hours or less, no matter the size of the home, apartment, or condo.

By

Pauline Irene Stacey

Hasmark
PUBLISHING
INTERNATIONAL

Hasmark Publishing
www.hasmarkpublishing.com

Permission should be addressed in writing to pauline@paulineirenestacey.com

Editor: Harshita Sharma
harshita@hasmarkpublishing.com

Cover Design: Anne Karklins
anne@hasmarkpublishing.com

Book Design: Amit Dey
amit@hasmarkpublishing.com

ISBN 13: 978-1-77482-044-5
ISBN 10: 1774820447

DEDICATION

This book is dedicated to everyone who dislikes housecleaning or just does not have enough time to spend doing weekly housecleaning chores.

Now you can take back your precious time to do what you like, and still have a clean home. Go spend time with your family, your friends, and most importantly, with yourself. Enjoy your weekend!

CONTENTS

INTRODUCTION

*L*ay your housecleaning blues to rest; I am here to rescue you from drudgery. You will use these tips and techniques for the rest of your life and will pass them on to family and friends.

Unless you are a part of the elite few who can hire a maid or a cleaning company for the rest of your life, you absolutely must read this book. Make it a part of your gift list for that bride-to-be, a child going off to college, or anyone starting off on his or her own. You will never again clean your house the same way; you will have an entirely new technique and a whole new attitude!

In this fast-paced world of "hurry up" and "needed it yesterday" attitudes, anytime someone offers us advice on how to speed up a task, we listen intently. Most often that advice does not enhance our lives in any other way except to give us a tad more time to squeeze in another task. This book has time-saving advice to increase the quality of your personal life.

How many painful hours do you spend cleaning your house during the week? More importantly, how many hours per week do you spend *thinking* about it?

Go ahead, start getting excited about this time-saving, money-saving, sanity-saving technique about a subject that most people dread.

Chapter 1

WHY DO WE HATE HOUSECLEANING?

My late Dad always said that any job is easy when you have the right tools. He was a painter. I wonder if he realized the impact of that statement when it comes to ordinary, everyday chores.

Housecleaning is a subject that most people do not look forward to even thinking about, much less doing on a daily or weekly basis. So, what are your options when it comes to housecleaning?

Hire someone to come on a weekly or bi-weekly basis.

Wait to do it until the dust pile is high enough that it can be measured with a ruler.

Use up one of the only two days that you have off from work every week.

Find a positive, efficient, scientific, and motivating way that will take only a couple of hours per week.

This book introduces the fourth choice. This is no joke. It is completely possible that anyone can change this dreaded chore that seems to consume our mind, as well as our time, into a challenging, more "upbeat" task that will take only a couple of hours out of your week. You no longer have to set aside one entire day for cleaning. You no longer need to refuse an invitation to go out in order to stay home and clean. I am sure you feel that this seems too good to be true. I absolutely promise you that it's not.

The method on which I have based my idea is a combination of two theories: scientific process and psychological process.

SCIENTIFIC PROCESS: This theory comes from a subject that has been studied for hundreds of years. Managers and business owners have spent years conducting experiments on how to get more production from their workers. The results of these experiments show that specialization (one person doing one task at a time) brought flow and speed to a process. For example, in a factory where seven tasks had to be performed on one product, instead of one person doing all seven tasks, that person would perform only one task on the product and then move it down the assembly line for the next step. In housecleaning, it is quite common for people to spend an hour or more in one room. When we separate each task (i.e., cleaning, organizing, putting things away, doing dishes, doing laundry, etc.) you will see that only minutes are spent in each room. We will discuss these steps later in detail.

PSYCHOLOGICAL PROCESS: The second theory that I have based my idea on is the power of positive thinking. I have spent hundreds of hours listening to self-motivational tapes, CDs, YouTube videos, and reading and listening to self-motivational books. Now, I have come to the realization that no matter who the author is or what the subject is, the bottom line is that positive energy **always** gets the job done better and faster. Psychologically, cleaning is a "dirty" job that no one likes. Why do you think it is that people who own a cleaning business make so much money? They are doing a job that NO ONE likes to do. But what if you could find a way to take the negative thoughts away from this job? We will discuss this, too, in detail.

Until you have experienced it, I do not believe that you can imagine the fantastic feeling of stepping out of the house for a couple of hours or spending the day at work and coming home to neat vacuum lines in the carpet, shiny floors, dust-free furniture, and spotless windows and mirrors. This is the experience of having a cleaning service. What an awesome feeling to realize that not only do you not have to do the cleaning, but you do not have to spend the rest of the week thinking about it! The guilt of sitting down watching TV while you "pig out" or run the kids all over town, never having a moment for yourself, or having to apologize to your friends and family about how busy you are, no longer exists.

If you make a sincere effort to follow and practice my suggestions, this dreaded humdrum chore can be turned into an almost effortless, challenging weekly task. Enjoy your clean house, and most of all, enjoy your newly found freedom!

Chapter 2

THE PROPER FRAME
OF MIND

The Attitude: Like everything in life, how you set yourself up to think about anything greatly affects how you approach it, as well as its outcome. If you go to work every day with a bad attitude, chances are that you are not going to have a particularly good day. *You* have the power to decide what kind of attitude you are going to have about all situations in your life. Housecleaning is no exception. Follow these suggestions to help you have a more positive attitude about cleaning your house, and a better experience.

The Clothes: We tend to think that because we are dealing with dirt, we must put on our grungiest jeans, old T-shirt, pull our hair back in a ponytail and, of course, wear no make-up. There's something to be said about those old TV commercials with the housewife in an evening gown washing the floor. No one looks forward to a job that they would be embarrassed to be seen doing. There really is NO reason for not being able to look presentable while you are cleaning your house.

In several years of my housecleaning business, not once have I ever ruined any of my clothes while cleaning. (Note: If you choose to use bleach, be careful.)

The best advice that I can give to you about this topic is to dress in something that you would wear if you were going to lunch with a friend. You do not have to wear your best outfit, just something that you can move comfortably in and that if a friend were to come knocking on your door while you were smack in the middle of cleaning, you would feel good enough about the way you look to drop everything, wash your hands, and walk out of the house.

The Atmosphere: Have you ever found yourself in a traffic jam without your car radio working or listening to the news and the traffic report during rush hour? You get so stressed out thinking about the jam and how much later it is going to make you. It is not a pleasant experience. On the other hand, being in a traffic jam while listening to your favorite music makes all the difference. You find yourself tapping your fingers and toes and singing along. Time does not seem to pass as slowly, and the next thing you know, the traffic is moving again. While cleaning, take this opportunity to listen to your favorite music and do not be afraid to turn it up! (If there are other people in the house while you are cleaning and they complain about the music, tell them that when *they* clean, they too can blast their favorite music.)

The Cleaning Cloths: Just as your clothes make a difference, so do your "rags." It is against all of the new "rules" to use stained, cut-up, old rags for dusting or cleaning. Imagine dusting with blue, green, yellow, or pink cloths—it puts a smile on your face, doesn't it?

Go to any discount linen shop or department store and buy face cloth-size towels of your favorite color only. In addition, today, microfiber cleaning cloths do a great job. They come in several beautiful colors, and different colors can represent different cleaning purposes. Buy several of them so that you do not have to worry about running out if you did not wash your cleaning cloths last week. Personally, I like to let my cleaning cloths pile up before I do a load of wash. Keep these cleaning cloths separate for house-cleaning only. Buy a stack for the rest of the family, but do not mix them with "your" cleaning cloths.

Chapter 3

THE RIGHT TOOLS

With so many cleaning products on the market, how do you really know which ones are the best or most effective? Trial and error and recommendations by friends and family. Since I had the opportunity to go through products quickly, I have tried several different products over the years. In addition, cleaning so many different types and styles of furniture, appliances, floors, etc., has helped me determine the best product for overall cleaning. If you find a product that you are satisfied with, by all means, stick with it. Remember, *you* should be happy.

A new term that has popped up over the past few years is "green cleaning." I could write another book about the subject of using environmentally-friendly cleaning products and the use of disposable cleaning products. The subject can get pretty complicated and scientific. There is plenty of information on the web about product recommendations and warnings. I am going to stick to my subject of "how to clean" rather than tackle "what to use." Suffice to say, you can do your own homework and speak with friends and family about what works best for them. If you do find a product that you just love and want to share, you can do so by visiting my website, www.PaulineIreneStacey.com, and submitting your suggestion. I will add it to my Facebook page as well.

Let us begin with the important suggestion of how to carry your cleaning products. You will need two buckets. One should fit into the other. All your cleaning products will always be kept together. Never separate them. You will understand why this is so important as we progress. In the bottom bucket, you will keep several cloths (remember: only your favorite colors). This helps break the suction when you need to separate the buckets. The top bucket will hold your products. The following items are what should be in your cleaning bucket.

PRODUCTS

Dusting Product: Picks up dust (wax-free)

Electronics Dusting Product/Antistatic dusting spray (optional): Safely cleans external housing on electronic equipment (oil- and wax-free)

Multipurpose Cleaner (spray bottle): For windows, glass, countertops, etc.

Soap Scum Remover: For showers and tubs (not every week)

Instant Mildew Remover: For showers and tubs (not every week)

Floor Cleaner

Stainless Steel Polish: For kitchen appliances

Chrome Polish (Cleaner/Polisher for chrome): Removes greasy film and watermarks, resists fingerprints and streaking. Some stainless steel polishes also work on chrome.

Scrubbing Cleaning Powder: For tubs, toilets, and sinks

Paper Towels: White only (no lint or film)

Inexpensive Tall Kitchen Bags

Scraper for stuck-on grime on floors and Razor Blade for stuck-on grime on mirrors and windows

Flexible-Handle Toothbrush

Rubber Gloves: Loose fitting to slide on and off easily

Multi-color Microfiber Cleaning Cloths

Two Cleaning Sponges: Different colors for different purposes. For instance, blue for toilet bowls. (It's easier to remember, "blue for bowls.")

EQUIPMENT:

Floor Vac: For floors. NO brooms! Must fit easily into corners and other small, tough-to-reach areas where dirt/dust accumulates.

Upright Vacuum: No tank or central vacuums

Floor Mop: Simple and easy to use

As we continue, you will understand why these products and supplies are an absolute must. (Note: Wearing an apron to carry your supplies in for the convenience of handiness is not practical. You need to move freely to move quickly. Items will fall out of the apron when bending over or possibly even on your clothes. If you would like, you may pour a portion of your products into smaller containers to allow for more room in your bucket and make it lighter to carry. However, make sure when switching containers that they have different color tops or shapes, so that when cleaning, each product is easily identifiable and not mistaken for another product. **Always** mark the container with the product that it contains.

Chapter 4

READY, SET, GO!

Now that you have your mind set and your bucket prepared, you are ready to begin. At first, you will be a little slower until you get used to the process and routine, which should take only two to three times. The absolute biggest taboo on your selected cleaning day and time is putting things away or "straightening up" the house. The number one reason that people hate cleaning is that it seems to take forever, and the reason is that they *mix chores*. This is the scientific factor that I referred to in the beginning. While cleaning, do not do laundry, do not pick up toys and put them in their proper places, and do not wash the dishes. We get too easily sidetracked, and it ends up taking us forever to get the "cleaning" done. Remember the scientific side to this cleaning method—do *one* task at a time, which in this case is to clean.

Have you ever found yourself starting to clean the kitchen when you find something on the counter that belongs in the bathroom? You walk across the house to put it away in its proper drawer, but then you notice that drawer is a mess, and you begin straightening it up. Too much time has passed since you began cleaning the kitchen. Now you have lost momentum and get frustrated about how long "cleaning" takes. Your options are to straighten up the house the night before (or just before you start cleaning), or to leave everything exactly where it is and clean around it.

If option two bothers you, remember that you still have option one. With option two, at least you will get the house clean, which you probably would not do if you waited until all things were put into their proper place.

Everything that goes up must come down, even dust. Therefore, when cleaning you must always follow the "top to bottom" rule. Clean everything from the top to the bottom. When you wipe the top first, whatever falls from your dust cloth will fall onto a section not wiped yet. This prevents having to clean anything twice or the possibility of leaving the dust or dirt behind. In this illustration, you would wipe the top of the picture frame and then the bottom lip of the inside of the frame, then the top of the computer desk, and then the shelves from top to bottom.

Do not move things if you do not feel like it. You do not necessarily need to move everything every week. Go with your mood and feelings. If you want to take the time to move things, do so. If not, do not bother. No one will know and no one will care.

Every house, of course, is different, as well as the individual who is doing the cleaning. Just keep in mind that these are basic and general guidelines designed to help you get the job done in the shortest time possible. Always feel free to make whatever adjustments and additions you feel are necessary for your situation, keeping in mind that you stick to the system of doing only the cleaning and nothing else.

Chapter 5

WHERE DO I BEGIN?

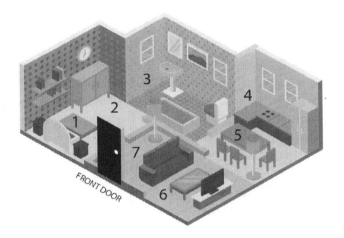

The concept is to work your way out of the house moving backwards, in the direction of the front door. The theory is that you are moving the dust and dirt out of the house. In addition, this prevents you from walking in a room that has already been cleaned. We will discuss how to move around in a room later. Looking at this illustration, my suggestion would be to begin in room #4 (the farthest room from the front door), then progress to room #5, room #6, #3, #2, #1, and then room #7 (the central area in front of the front door) and out. Of course, you can change the path and do what comes naturally to you. Just remember to work your way out of the house towards the front door. To help make it more understandable, visualize the dirt moving out of the room and out the front door.

If you have an upstairs, always begin there. Start with the room farthest away from the staircase. Follow all the procedures described above for upstairs and then repeat downstairs. Once you start cleaning upstairs, you should not have to go downstairs for any reason until you are finished cleaning, except for floors. All floors are done at the same time in the last step. (We will discuss this further.) Read on!

 Separate your buckets, one with the cleaning products in it (the top bucket), and the other with your cleaning cloths. Take out your floor sweeper, vacuum, and mop. Leave them all in a central place downstairs, but out of the way. If you start upstairs, take only the cleaning buckets with you. Put the bucket in a central location, accessible from all rooms. Take one trash bag, open it up, and lay it on the floor next to the bucket. The reason for leaving it open is that you can throw the used paper towels in it from where you are standing instead of wasting time walking over to the trash bag each time you need to discard a paper towel. If you miss from inside the room, no worries—you can pick it up once you leave the room and put it in the trash bag. This ends up being kind of a fun game to test your basketball skills.

KEEP YOUR SUPPLIES CLEAN. One of the best tips that I can give you for cleaning is to always make sure that you are cleaning with a clean cloth, whether it is a cloth for dusting, paper towel for windows or mirrors, or a sponge for counter-tops. If your towel has dirt on it, all you're doing is moving the dirt, not eliminating the dirt. In the case of a sponge, all that you can do to avoid this problem is to constantly rinse your sponge. Even though this may seem time-consuming, the only alternative is to waste wiping strokes in order to move the dirt, hair, and lint to the edge of the counter or surface, which is much more frustrating.

Fold the cloth or paper towel into quarters. As soon as the side that you are using is dirty, fold it again so that it is now in eighths. Once this side is dirty, do not turn it over; you will be exposing the dirt to your skin, which you should always try to avoid.

Whenever cleaning, always avoid skin contact with dirt or cleaning products. (Always use a good-quality hand cream before and after cleaning.) Now, open up the cloth so that it is in half and fold it over so that the dirty sides are facing each other and it is in quarters again. Both sides of the cloth should be clean. Then repeat.

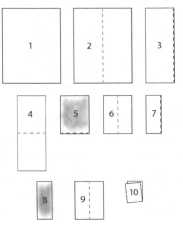

When dusting, you may go so far as to open the cloth completely and repeat the folding process. For paper towels, it is better to replace, as the towel is usually

Pauline's Pearls

saturated by this time. After learning this trick, you will never again wrinkle up or "ball up" a cloth or paper towel. This method of folding is much more productive and efficient, as well as conservative—you use less cloths and paper towels and hence, *less time* changing them.

Chapter 6

DUSTING

*B*egin dusting, keeping in mind the theory of one task at a time. Carry your cloth and dusting product to the room farthest away from the front door (or staircase, for that matter). Start at the right (or left) of the room's door, working your way around the room in a circle and back out of the room. Spray your dust cloth, not the furniture. This helps prevent any product buildup. (If the surface is exceptionally dirty, you may spray it and rub well.) Dust everything reachable from top to bottom, including frames, furniture, and baseboards.

This next suggestion may seem awkward at first, but it is one of my favorite cleaning hacks.

It is easy to catch on to and extremely handy. While dusting, hold the dust can between your legs. This frees up both your hands, preventing you from having to keep picking up and putting down the can on another surface, which may require you to take steps to keep picking it up. One hand can move things and the

other can dust. It makes the dusting portion of cleaning super smooth and quick.

If you are dealing with a lot of pet hair, it would be easier if you remove the pet hair first with a feather duster, using quick, short strokes. The hair will fall to the floor or carpet, which you will pick up when vacuuming. Initially, this may seem like twice the work, but believe me, trying to move hair when you are dusting does not work. The hair clings to the cloth at first and then falls off onto the other surfaces while you dust, making you change your cloth frequently.

Move on to the next rooms using the same process—only dusting. When your cloth is used up or close to it, change it while leaving one room and passing the bucket on your way to another room. Start a pile for dirty cloths near your bucket. Your goal is to not have to leave a room once in it, whether to change cloths or get cleaning products. This eliminates a lot of time wasted walking back and forth and keeps the flow and momentum going.

Now your entire house is dusted.

Next, take your trash bag into every room that has a small trash can that needs to be emptied. When finished emptying all cans, leave the trash bag open near the bucket in the hallway where you placed all your supplies and equipment.

Chapter 7

MIRRORS AND GLASS

The next step is mirrors and glass. Take your paper towels and glass cleaner. I recommend using cleaning cloths specifically designed for glass. They work really well and do not leave streaks and smudges. Folding the towel as previously mentioned, you may spray the towel or the surface. It is recommended by mirror manufacturers that you do not spray the mirror's surface, because as time goes on, you could damage the mirror. However, sometimes that is the only way to clean the mirror well (especially in bathrooms).

At this time, you are working only in the rooms that you have just dusted. Do not go into bathrooms or the kitchen yet. When you have used up your towel, just throw the towel from the door of the room into the trash bag or start a pile of dirty cleaning cloths on the side of the bucket (or at least in the vicinity). Again, the point is to save time by not wasting steps walking over to the trash each time. Do not be afraid to use plenty of towels. Only a clean, dry towel will clean a surface well. Do not forget to clean the television glass. You will be amazed when you look at the paper towel or cloth the first time you do this. Use a product designed for electronics on televisions, computers, stereos, etc. This is also the time to do the inside of sliding glass doors or windows, only if they are dirty. If they look clean, leave it. Do not go outside. It may drive you crazy to clean the inside only, but that is another project for another day.

Chapter 8

BATHROOMS

The bathroom is where you are going to have to invest the most amount of time. Although some of these steps may seem time-consuming, I promise you that I have perfected this stage to a science, and you will be thrilled with the results. Always remember, however, that if you do find a faster and/or better way, use it. This is all about you and what it takes to make this experience pleasant for you. Every bathroom is different. After a couple of times, you will learn to adjust these general guidelines to your unique situation.

Take your bucket and trash bag over to the farthest bathroom in the house, leaving them just outside the door. Empty the trash. Before you begin cleaning, there are a few things you can do to make the process easier. If there are any throws or area rugs on the bathroom floor (this also applies to any other room), shake the rug gently **low to the floor**, just where the rug lies. This step saves plenty of time by not having to walk around the house to go outside and then back inside. If you just cannot bring yourself to shake the rugs in the room, go ahead and shake it outside, but take all rugs with you at the same time to avoid going outside for each rug in the house. The dirt from the rug will be picked up when you vacuum the floor. Roll up the rug and place it just outside the bathroom, out of the way. Next, move any towels that will be in your way. Move the counter items to one side, so that when you are ready to clean that area everything is out of the way, which will help you move quickly through the process.

Start with the toilet bowl. There are products on the market that may seem much more convenient than my suggestion. However, those disposable products are designed for "in between" weekly cleanings. They clean only the inside of the bowl. You will see that my suggestion is the most effective and convenient way to thoroughly clean and disinfect the entire toilet bowl once a week. If there are males in the family, you will see why this is so important the first time you do this. Pour a portion of your all-purpose cleaner and scrubbing powder product into the bowl. Using the blue sponge that I recommended for toilets only, constantly rinsing the sponge in bowl water, wipe the inside of the bowl, inside the lid, outside the lid, the inside and outside of the cover, and the outside of the bowl, as well as the bottom edges. The flexible-handle toothbrush is perfect for around the toilet seat cover bolts. Flush the water when finished.

The bath/shower can be simple or can take several steps to get it looking squeaky clean, depending on the type of tile, whether you have shower doors or curtains, or if there is lots of chrome, etc. Water spots are the most difficult to deal with. Start with the shower first. If the shower is still wet, the best way to begin cleaning it is to completely dry the shower first. Take a dirty hand towel or bath towel, drop it on the tile floor and step on it, moving it around under your feet to dry the floor. Then, depending on how wet that cloth is, use it or another cloth to quickly dry the walls. A dry shower is much easier to clean, especially when it comes to sweeping the hairs off the floor.

Using a soap scum remover, spray only the dirty tiles and then wipe them clean with your sponge, remembering to rinse often, even if you have to keep walking over to the sink. This is the one instance when walking back and forth is okay, as it is necessary. It may seem like a waste of time, but you will use more time trying to fix the streaks and re-wiping later. (This is the reason that you save the sinks for last.) This product works well on chrome also. The glass doors will come out best using something more specifically formulated for glass. A lime and a rust remover are great for bathrooms.

There are a couple of steps involved in getting your glass doors looking their best, but it is worth the effort. If, however, your doors have not been kept up with and have caked-on water spots, take heart in knowing that with a weekly cleaning, it will improve and possibly all go away as time goes on. If the fumes bother you, spray the entire door and then wipe it immediately, as the product works just as well as when you let it sit. Let the doors dry while you finish the bathroom. We will get back to them to take care of any remaining product left after drying.

Next is the chrome. Use a product that not only shines the chrome, but cleans it too. You will be amazed at how this step puts the professional looking touch on your bathroom. If you have shower doors, do not forget the chrome edging.

Saving the sinks for last, next are the countertops. If there are strands of hair on the counter, give it a quick "dry wipe" to remove them. Then spray and wipe down

the counter with your all-purpose cleaner. Do not worry about getting the strands on the floor— you will pick them up when you vacuum. Wipe the counter, and just before you are ready to rinse your sponge, wipe the sink while the sponge has product on it, and then rinse. You may have to rinse your sponge several times in this area, but it is worth it. Your bathroom will sparkle and shine when you are done.

Before you put items back into place on the counter is the best time to clean the mirror. Otherwise, your counter items will make it difficult to work around and you will end up missing spots on the mirror and, of course, using more precious time. Use your razor blade to instantly remove any stuck-on grime. Now, replace your items and work on the other side of the counter, as well as that side of the mirror. If there is any other glass or mirrors in the bathroom, now is the time to clean them. Do not forget to go back to your shower doors. Now that they are dry from the first step, you can wipe them with your all-purpose or glass cleaner. This step removes the streaks and smears left behind from the soap scum remover. Move on to the next bathrooms following the same procedures. Once you have finished all bathrooms, you can start getting excited. Only the kitchen and floors are left.

Chapter 9

KITCHENS

Kitchens are generally easy to do because they are usually kept up with on a daily basis. You may begin with the kitchen table and then go on to the countertops, following the procedure you used in the bathroom, moving items from side to side. Be sure to move small appliances so that you can get the crumbs from behind things that you generally do not move during the week. Remember to move around the room in a circle, saving the sink for last. Rinse your sponge often. Use anything that has a germicide in it to clean the kitchen.

Wipe only the outside of your kitchen appliances. If you want to clean inside toasters, refrigerators, etc., remember to make this another day's project. However, do wipe the inside of your microwave. (Hint: If you cover everything you cook in the microwave, cleaning is a snap! If there is dried food stuck to the inside walls, boil a cup of water inside the microwave. The steam from the water will loosen the food.[1]) Clean all items that need

---

[1] If the inside is really dirty the first time you clean it, you may also clean it by mixing equal parts water and baking soda. Dab with a paper towel to scrub microwave.

glass cleaner at the same time. Wipe the outside of the cupboard doors only if they are dirty. Do not clean all the cupboards—only spot wipe. Save this time-consuming chore of cupboard cleaning for a different type of cleaning day, like spring and fall cleaning, or maybe the same day you do the outside of your windows and sliding glass doors. Do not forget to use a product specifically for stainless steel appliances. This really leaves the finishing-touch look in the kitchen.

Chapter 10

CARPETS

The last step is all the floors, including the carpets. Do all the vacuuming first. When vacuuming, choose a plug farthest away from the door that you are entering. Be sure that it is not at an angle, so that when you pull on the cord from across the room, you do not bend the plug. When finished vacuuming, give the plug a nice sturdy yank from across the room and the plug will come out of the wall outlet, allowing you to finish pulling the cord toward you. This little time-saver is fun as well as helpful, because you do not have to walk over the vacuum lines; that is impressive for a room that you do not generally use or want company to see before you use.

Work from the back of the room out towards the entrance, walking backwards. Use one hand to push the vacuum and one hand to hold the cord, so that you can control it. This keeps footprints off the vacuum lines for a fresh-looking job.

I cannot emphasize enough the importance of using a simple upright vacuum. I realize that it is a status symbol to have an expensive, fancy vacuum. However, after several years of experiencing both versions, I can tell you that lugging around a tank vacuum or the hose of a central vac system is not necessarily fast, efficient, or glamorous.

This is one of those psychological factors that come into play. Lugging around this bulky equipment does not make a person excited about doing a job or chore. The point is to make things as simple and easy as possible to do an efficient and effective job. Just make sure that you know exactly what you are buying. There are a lot of vacuums out there that only "surface clean." You want something that is going to suck up what is in the bottom layer of the carpet as well. This will prolong the life of your carpet. Also make sure that you use vacuum cleaner bags that trap micro dust particles from re-entering the air. If you want to use a bulky system like a central vac or tank, do that maybe once a month. Keep the weekly cleaning lighter and quicker.

If you enjoy the smell of carpet freshener, feel free to use it before and even after vacuuming.

Chapter 11

FLOORS

*S*ticking to the subject of simple, the best way to "sweep" any floor type or size is to use an upright stick vacuum for floors. There are so many on the market today. You can visit <u>consumerreports.org</u> for suggestions. Most are inexpensive, lightweight, and powerful. You will be amazed at how fast and effective this tool makes "sweeping" floors of any size, especially if you have animals or children. This is an absolute must.

Use the same method as vacuuming—work from the back of the room towards the main entrance. Remember the beginning of the book, where I discussed that the theory is to move the dust and dirt out of the house. Always walk backwards whenever vacuuming or mopping.

Mopping the floors is the last step. This is another cleaning tool that has so many options today. You really have to find what works best for you. There are microfiber wet mops, spin mop systems, disposable pad systems, steam mop systems, spray mop systems, and many more. Do some research, and talk to family and friends to see what they like based on their experiences.

Maybe you can borrow theirs once to see if it is for you.

However, if you choose to use the simple "old fashioned" mop and bucket system, follow these directions.

Remove the clean cloths from the bottom bucket. Fill the bucket with water first to prevent bubbles. Add your floor cleaner after the bucket is halfway to ¾ full. Wear your gloves if you are manually squeezing your mop. The trick when mopping floors is to leave your mop fairly wet. Do not squeeze it dry. A very wet mop is much more effective on a dirty floor. Open doors or windows or put on ceiling fans to help decrease the drying time.

As always, work backwards out to the doorway, using long, even strokes. Keep your scraper in your hand to quickly scrape off any stuck-on grime. This eliminates stroking over and over again. Use the tiles as a guideline for which tiles have already been mopped. For instance, wipe three or four tiles across and down, doing a block of nine to twelve, before rinsing and moving on to the next section. Do all floors, rinsing your mop as needed, remembering to keep it wet. This step should be quite simple and quick.

A quick little tip: If you find it necessary, for whatever reason, to have to walk on the wet floor, put a dry cloth under each foot and kind of shuffle into the room and back out. This will keep footsteps off the wet floor and prevent you from slipping.

Chapter 12

CLEANUP

*Y*ou may empty your bucket of dirty water in a toilet bowl or outside on the lawn. If you choose to empty the dirty water in the toilet, do not forget to flush it after. Using one of your dirty cloths, wipe the inside bottom of the bucket clean and dry. Replace any clean cloths that you have not used back in the bottom of the bucket. Place the other bucket with the products into the bucket with the cloths. Now, your buckets are completely ready for next week, saving the effort and time of having to "get ready." Put your trash bag out with the garbage, replace area rugs, and enjoy the rest of your week in your professionally-cleaned home, for FREE!

Chapter 13

CONCLUSION

*L*ike everything else in life, we do not tend to like the things that we do not understand. Since cleaning is a topic no one ever taught us how to do, we get frustrated with not only having to do the job, but also with the time it takes, as we are doing more than one chore at a time. We mix cleaning with organizing, doing the dishes, doing laundry, putting things away, and other larger projects. Understanding that cleaning is a chore in itself is a great step towards getting it done in much less time.

I believe understanding that feeling good about the way you are dressed and using your favorite color cleaning cloths can go a long way to a better attitude about a chore we do not normally get enthusiastic about.

In addition, using the right tools and products is key to helping make the job easier and faster, and therefore more pleasant. Imagine an artist using cheap nylon brushes and low-quality paint for a painting, and then imagine the same artist using an exquisitely crafted sable-hair brush with rich pigmented oil paint. Not only does the final job look better, but the experience is much more pleasant as well.

A step-by-step system not only ensures you have a clean house, but also saves the precious time we all need. After following the system just a few times, it really will become second nature. The organized system takes the "thinking" out of the chore, which saves time. You know exactly what your next steps are. It also helps keep your mind on track—not getting distracted from cleaning when you start roaming around the house from room to room, putting things away.

The "rules" and tips in this book will forever be a part of your weekly cleaning routine. I am sure that you will want to share what you discovered with everyone you know, so they can take back their weekends, too.

BONUS 1:

Go to www.NoTimeToCleanListenToPauline.com to print out easy-to-follow outlines to take into each room. You can place the individual sheets in your cleaning bucket to follow a simple outline, so you do not have to remember what you read or take the book with you when you are cleaning. Just follow the steps for each room's outline. There's one sheet for each specific task/room.

BONUS 2:

Feel free to visit my website, www.PaulineIreneStacey.com, and submit any questions you have about cleaning. I will personally answer each question.

ABOUT THE AUTHOR

Pauline Irene Stacey

Pauline Irene Stacey grew up in Massachusetts. She lived in New York City when she was 18. She moved to South Florida for a year with her husband, who had just gotten out of the Navy. Wanting to be closer to her family, she moved back to Massachusetts. Then three years later, she went back to South Florida with her three-year-old daughter, in search of a better life.

As a single parent in her late twenties, Pauline earned a bachelor's degree in business management at Florida Atlantic University. She was highly active in extracurricular activities as president of a state chapter organization and a member of various other committees. She also taught religious education for five years.

After working for others in the cleaning business, the busy schedule made her realize that self-employment was the best decision for her. It became clear to her that with the management skills she was learning in college and the hands-on experience she had gained, she had the knowledge and the drive to start her own cleaning business. Since time is valuable, she had to find a way to do a great job in less time. She developed methods that allowed her to speed up the process while keeping her clients happy. She was so successful that the business continued for eight years. During this time, she perfected housecleaning to a science and discovered how to address the psychology behind many people disliking cleaning.

After leaving the business to become a teacher, she knew she had to share her expertise with all the other people in the world who hate cleaning, as well as those trying to balance a career and find time for their family. This book is her contribution to society to help people find a positive way to deal with the unpleasant chore of weekly housecleaning, allowing them to focus their energy and time on the activities that bring joy to their lives.

Pauline went on to earn her master's degree in environmental management. She is a former member of the Board of Directors of Florida Atlantic University's National Alumni Association for two consecutive terms. She has had several environmental papers published, including her master's thesis, *Ecotourism: A Tool for Conservation*, which was cited at an ecotourism conference in Belize.

In 2008, Pauline established her own environmental firm, Environmental Matters Contracting & Consulting, LLC, after spending almost two decades in corporate America and financing her own education.

She has been proactive in environmental advocacy through her nonprofit environmental work. She is passionate about water issues and works closely with local, state, and national legislators promoting a healthy Everglades ecosystem. She is a two-time Everglades Coalition Board Member, former Executive Coordinator of Everglades Coalition, former Board Member (elected twice for consecutive terms) and current member of the Friends of Arthur R. Marshall Loxahatchee National Wildlife Refuge, as well as the voting delegate for the Everglades Coalition.

Visit Pauline's website for more information:
www.paulineirenestacey.com

Facebook Pauline Irene Stacey
Instagram @paulineirenestacey
LinkedIn Pauline Stacey

**Feel free to share whatever is on your mind, including
thoughts, comments, suggestions – or ask any
question at all.
Pauline will personally answer.**
pauline@paulineirenestacey.com

Pauline's passion is to share with others her discoveries of
how to save time and money with practical solutions to
everyday common problems of keeping their home clean and
their lives organized.

Stay tuned for her next book in the series
"No Time To…? Listen To Pauline!"

Meanwhile, keep following for more *"Pauline's Pearls".

HEARTS to be HEARD

Giving a Voice to Creativity!

With every donation, a voice will be given to
the creativity that lies within the hearts of
our children living with diverse challenges.

By making this difference, children that may
not have been given the opportunity to have their
Heart Heard will have the freedom to create
beautiful works of art and musical creations.

Donate by visiting

HeartstobeHeard.com

We thank you.

Made in the USA
Columbia, SC
23 July 2021

42220743R00033